INTRODUCTION TO THEORY OF AUTOMATA & COMPILER DESIGN

BEGINNER'S HANDBOOK FOR DESIGNING FINITE STATE MACHINES USING AUTOMATA

AF664984

DAVID LIVINGSTON J

Copyright © David Livingston J
All Rights Reserved.

This book has been published with all efforts taken to make the material error-free after the consent of the author. However, the author and the publisher do not assume and hereby disclaim any liability to any party for any loss, damage, or disruption caused by errors or omissions, whether such errors or omissions result from negligence, accident, or any other cause.

While every effort has been made to avoid any mistake or omission, this publication is being sold on the condition and understanding that neither the author nor the publishers or printers would be liable in any manner to any person by reason of any mistake or omission in this publication or for any action taken or omitted to be taken or advice rendered or accepted on the basis of this work. For any defect in printing or binding the publishers will be liable only to replace the defective copy by another copy of this work then available.

Contents

SECTION I - Theory of Automata

CHAPTER ONE

Mathematical Background & Proofs

A set is a collectionof well defined objects. For example, all the students who enroll for a course named "Theory Of Computation" make up a set. All the elements of a set has common properties.

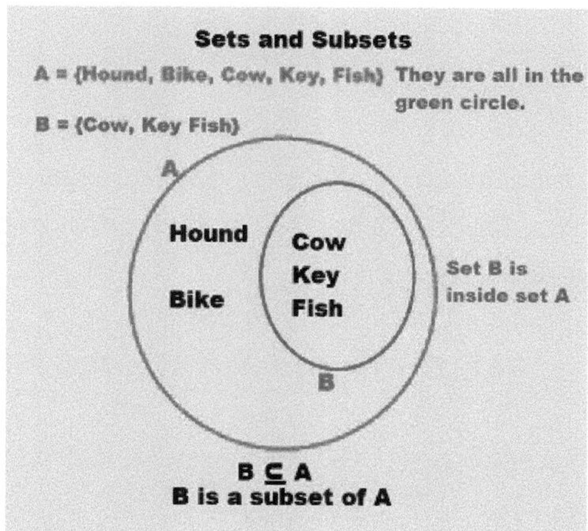

Fig. 1.1 Representing a Set and its Subset

Here is another Example. The set ofeven positive integer less than 20 can be expressed as:
E= {2,4,6,8,10,12,14,16,18}
Or
E= $\{x \mid x \text{ is even and } 0<x<20\}$

Finite and Infinite Sets:

A set is finite if it contains finite number of elements. Whereas, an infinite set has infinite number of elements in it. The number of elements in a set is called the **Cardinality** of set.

The cardinality of the set E defined above is |E|=9. An empty set has no element and is denoted by ϕ. A set named A is a **subset** of another set B if each element of A is also element of B and is denoted as A ⊆ B.

Set operations:

Union: The union operation on two sets results in a set consisting of elements from one of the two sets and possibly both. Union isdenoted by the symbol ∪.

Intersection: The intersection of two sets results in the collection of all commmon elements from both sets and is denoted by ∩.

Differences: The difference of two sets A and B, denoted by A-B, is the set of all elements that are in the set A but not in the set B.

Sequences:

A sequence of objects is a list of objects in some order. For example, the sequence 7,4,17 would be written as (7,4,17). In set the order does not matter but in sequence it does. Also, repetitionis not permitted in a set but is allowed in a sequence. Like set, sequence may be finite or infinite.

Relations and Functions

A binary relation on two sets A and B is a subset of A×B. For example, if A={1,3,9}, B={x,y}, then {(1,x),(3,y),(9,x)} is a binary relation on 2-sets.

A function is an object that setup an input-output relationship, i.e. a function takes an input and produces the required output. For example, a function f, with input x, and output y, we write f(x)=y. We also say that f maps x to y.

A binary relation r is an equivalence relation if R satisfies:

- R is reflexive, i.e. for every x, (x,x)ϵR.
- R is symmetric, i.e. for every x and y, (x,y)ϵR imlies (y,x) ϵR.
- R is transitive, i..e. for every x,y, and z, (x,y) ϵR and (y,z) ϵR imples (x,z) ϵR.

Closures Property of Sets:

Closures is an important relationship among sets and is a general tool for dealing with sets and relationship of many kinds. Let R be a binary relation on a set A. Then the reflexive closure of R is a relation R' such that :

- R' is reflexive (symmetric, transitive)
- R' ⊇ R.
- If R" is a reflexive relation containing R then R" ⊇ R

The Basic Concepts of Language

The basic terms that pervade the theory of automata include alphabets, strings, languages, etc. A language is a (possibly infinite) set of strings, all of which choose their symbols from some alphabet.

Alphabets (Represented by "Σ"):

An alphabet is a finite set of symbols. The symbols can be the letters such as {a, b, c}, bits {0, 1}, digits {0, 1, 2, 3... 9}, common characters like $, #, etc. The following is a two set of alphabets that may be used for forming an expression:

{0,1} – a Binary alphabets

{+, –, *} –Special symbols

Strings:

String is a finite sequence of symbols taken from some alphabet. E.g. 0110 is a string from binary alphabet. Strings are denoted by lower case letters. Automata helps us to identify the valid strings over a set of alphabets {a, b, c ... z}.

Empty String:

It is a string with zero occurrences of symbols. It is denoted by ε (epsilon).

Length of String:

The length of a string w, denoted by | w |, is the number of positions for symbols in w. We have for every string s, length (s) ≥ 0.

| ε | = 0 as empty string have no symbols.

| 0110 | = 4

Power of alphabet:

The set of all strings of certain length k from an alphabet is the kth power of that alphabet. i.e. Σk = {w / |w| = k}

If Σ = {0, 1}then,

- Σ0= {ε}

- $\Sigma 1 = \{0, 1\}$
- $\Sigma 2 = \{00, 01, 10, 11\}$
- $\Sigma 3 = \{000, 001, 010, 011, 100, 101, 110, 111\}$

Kleen Closure (*):

The set of all the strings over an alphabet Σ is called kleen closure of Σ & is denoted byΣ^*. Thus, kleen closure is set of all the strings over alphabet Σ with length 0 or more.

$\therefore \Sigma^* = \Sigma 0 \cup \Sigma 1 \cup \Sigma 2 \cup \Sigma 3 \cup$...............

For Example, if $A = \{0\}$

$A^* = \{0\text{^}n \mid n = 0, 1, 2, ...\}$.

Positive Closure (+):

The set of all the strings over an alphabet Σ, except the empty string is called positive closure and is denoted by $\Sigma +$.

$\therefore \Sigma + = \Sigma 1 \cup \Sigma 2 \cup \Sigma 3 \cup$...............

Operations on Strings

A language L over an alphabet Σ is subset of all the strings that can be formed out of Σ; i.e. a language is subset of kleen closure over an alphabet Σ; $L \subseteq \Sigma^*$.

In other words, a set of strings chosen from Σ^* defines a language. Here are some examples of languages:

- The set of all strings over $\Sigma = \{0, 1\}$ with equal number of 0's & 1's is this:
    - $L = \{\varepsilon, 01, 0011, 000111, ...\}$
- φ is an empty language & is a language over any alphabet.
- {ε} is a language consisting of only empty string.
- Set of binary numbers whose value is a prime:
    - $L = \{10, 11, 101, 111, 1011, ...\}$

Concatenation of Strings:

Let x & y be strings then xy denotes concatenation of x & y, i.e. the string formed by making a copy of x & following it by a copy of y.

More precisely, if x is the string of i symbols as x = a1a2a3...ai & y is the string of j symbols as y = b1b2b3...bj then xy is the string of i + j symbols as xy = a1a2a3...aib1b2b3...bj. For example:

x = 000

y = 111

xy = 000111 &

yx = 111000

Note:_'ε' is identity for concatenation; i.e. for any w, εw = wε = w.

Suffix of a string:

A string s is called a suffix of a string w if it is obtained by removing 0 or more leading symbols in w. For example,

w = abcd

s = bcd is suffix of w.

here s is proper suffix if s ≠ w.

Prefix of a string:

A string s is called a prefix of a string w if it is obtained by removing 0 or more trailing symbols of w. For example;

w = abcd

s = abc is prefix of w.

Here, *s* is a proper suffix, i.e. *s* is proper suffix if s ≠ w.

Substring:

A string s is called substring of a string w if it is obtained by removing 0 or more leading or trailing symbols in w. It is a proper substring of w if s ≠ w.

For example, if s is a string then Substr(s, i, j) is substring of s beginning at i-th position & ending at j-th position both inclusive.

Problem:

When the strings of a language are to be interpreted in some way, the question of whether a string is in the language is sometimes called a problem.

A problem can be defined as a matter of deciding whether a given string is a member of some particular language or not. In other words, if Σ is an alphabet, and L is a language over Σ, then the problem on L is defined like this:

- Given a string w in Σ*, decide whether or not w is in L

Different Ways of Proving a Theorem

A formal proof is a proof in which every logical inference has been checked all the way back to the fundamental axioms of mathematics. All the intermediate logical steps are supplied, without exception. No appeal is made to intuition, even if the translation from intuition to logic is routine. Thus, a formal proof is less intuitive, and yet less susceptible to logical errors.

Deductive Proof

This basic method of proof proceeds by listing statements that are either given to be true, or that follow logically from some of the previous statements.

This is the basic method of proof that proceeds from a sequence of initial statements, called the **hypothesis** or the given statement (s), the truth of which leads us to a conclusion statement.

The theorem that is proved when we go from a hypothesis H to a conclusion C is the statement of the form "if H the C", we say that C is deducted from H. Here is theorem to prove using deductive method:

If x>4, then 2^x > x^2

Proving If-Then Statements:

There are other theorems of the form "if (something) then (something else)." The statement or statement(s) following the "if" are the hypohesis, and what follows "then" is the conclusion. Deductive proofs of if-then statements begin with the hypothesis, and continue with statements that follow logically from the hypothesis and previous statements, until the conclusion is proved as one of the statmenets.

Proving If-And-Only-If Statements:

There are other theorems of the form "(something) if and only if (something else)." They are proved by showing if-then statements in both directions. A similar kind of theorem claims the equality of the sets described in two different ways; these are proved by showing that each of the two sets is contained in the other.

Proving the Contrapositive

Sometimes, it is easier to prove a statement of the form "if H then C" by proving the equivalent statement "if not C then not H." The latter is called the contrapositive of the former. Thus, the contrapositive fo the statement "if H then C" is "If not C then not H."

A statement and its contrapositive are either both true or both false, so we can prove either to prove the other. There are four cases to consider in the if-then form of a theorem:

1. H and C both are true
2. H true and C false
3. C true and H false
4. H and C both are false

There is only one way to make an if-then statment false: the hypothesis must be true and the conclusion false, as in case 2. But "not C" is true exactly when C is false, and "not H" is false exactly when H is true.

Proof by Contradiction:

Sometimes, it is more convenient to prove a statement "if H then C" by proving "if H and not C" in order to prove that something known to be is false. A proof of this type os called proof by contradiction.

Counter Examples:

Sometimes we are asked to show that a certain statement is not true. If the statement has one or more parameters, then we can show that it is false as a generality by providing just one counter example, that is, one assignement of values to the parameters that makes the statment false.

Inductive Proof

A statment that has an integer parameter n can often be proved by induction on n. We prove that the statement is true for a finite number of cases for particular values of n, and then prove the inductive step that says:

if the statment is true for values upto n, then it is true for n+1

Structural Induction:

In some situations, the theorem to be proved inductively is about some recursively defined construct, such as trees. We may prove a theorem about the constructed objects by induction on the number of steps used in its construction. This type of induction is referred to as structural.

CHAPTER TWO

Introduction to Theory of Computation & Automata

Theory of Computation is a branch of Computer Science that deals with how efficiently problems can be solved using a computing machine. The pupose of learning Theory of Computation is to develop formal mathematical models of computation that reflect real-world computers.

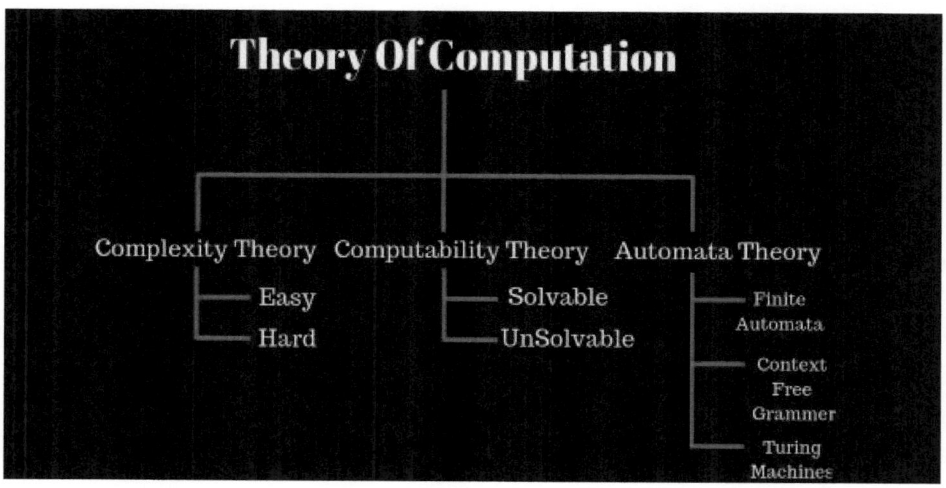

Fig. 2.1 Different Areas of Study in Theory of Computation

Theory of Computation has three breanches of study namely Complexity Theory, Compuational Theory and Automata Theory. **Complexity theory** deals with identifying the hardness of a problems. It helps us to find the level of complexity of a computation model. **Computational theory** is an area of study that deals with what can and what can't be computed by a computation model.

Automata Theory:

Automata theory is the study of abstract machines (or more appropriately, abstract 'mathematical' machines or systems) and the computational problems that can be solved using these machines. These abstract machines are called **automata.**

Automata theory helps us in answering the question: "what can a computer do at all? " This type of study is called "**decidability**" and the problems that can be solved by a computer are called "**decidable probelms.**"

The study that answers the question: "what can a computer do efficiently?" is called "**intractability**" and the problems that can be solved by a computer in polynomial time are called "**tractable probelms.**"

Brief of History of Automata:

Before there were computers, in the 1930's, A. Turing studied an abstract machine called **Turing Machine** that had all the capabilities of today's computers to some extent. His goal was to describe precisely the boundary between what a computing machine could do and what it could not do.

Later in 1940's and 1950's, simple kinds of machines called **Finite Automata** were introduced by a number of researchers. In late 1950's the linguist N. Chomsky begun the study of **formal Grammar** which are closely related to automata. In 1969 S. Cook extended Turing's study of what could and what couldn't be computed and classified problems into two types: Tractable and Intractable.

Abstract Model:

An abstract model is a model of computer system (considered either as hardware or software) constructed to allow a detailed and precise analysis of how the computer system works. Such a model usually consists of input, output and operations that can be performed and so can be thought of as a processor. E.g. an abstract machine that models a banking system can have operations like deposit, withdraw, transfer, etc.

Finite Automata and Its Types

Finite Automata is a state machine that comprehensively captures all possible states and transitions that a machine can take while responding to a stream (sequence) of input symbols. It is a useful computational model for building hardware or software that involve states and transitions among states in response to given inputs.

Some of the applications of Finite Automata are as follows:

1. Design and analyse the behavior of **digital circuits**
2. Design and implement **lexical analyzer**, a part of the compiler, that breaks the input text into logical units such as identifiers, keywords and punctuations
3. Design a **text processor** that can scan large bodies of text or web pages to find occurence of certain words, phrases or other patterns in them.

The main motivation behind the study of automata theory is to develop models that can descibe and analyse the dynamic behavior of discrete systems. The term "automata" is originated from the term "automaton" which is closely related to "automation" means "system that can be realized using a machine"

The reason for having finite number of states in a finite automata is that a system with finite states can be implemented with a fixed set of resources. For instance, a system with finite number of states can be implemented in a hardware as a circuit, or it can be implemented as a software in a program that can make decisions using the limited amount of data available.

Five Tuple Notation of Finite Automata:

Finite Automata (FA) is an abstract model that describes the behavior of a finite state machine. It can be used to model the behavior of a digital computer using **five elements** called **tuples.** Basically, a finite automata has a set of states and rules for moving from one state to another but it depends upon the applied input symbol for its operation. The following figure shows the structure of a finite automata:

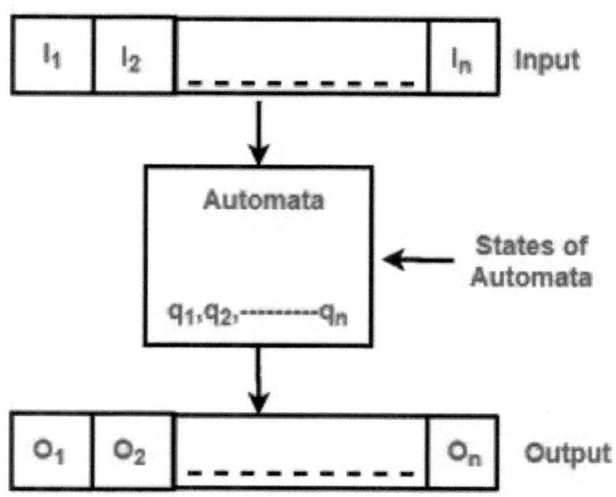

Fig. 2.2 Basic Structure of a Finite Automata

Here is the five tuple notation used for defining a Finite Automata:

$$\{ Q, \Sigma, q, F, \delta \}$$

where **Q** : Finite set of states; **Σ** : set of Input Symbols; **q** : Initial state; **F** : set of Final States; **δ** : Transition Function.

Finite Automata can be classified into **Deterministic Finite Automata** (DFA) and **Nondeterministic Finite Automata** (NFA).

Deterministic Finite Automata (DFA):

DFA consists of a set of 5 tuples {Q, Σ, q, F, δ}, where **Q** is the set of all states, **Σ** represents the set of input symbols (Symbols which machine takes as input), **q** is the Initial state (Starting state of a machine), **F** stands for set of final state and **δ** denotes a set of Transition Function, defined as δ : Q X Σ --> Q.

In DFA, for a particular input character, the machine may change its state from the current state to any one of the other states in the machine. A transition function is defined on every state for every input symbol. Moreover, null (or ε) move is not allowed in DFA, i.e., DFA cannot change its state without any input character.

For example, below DFA with Σ = {0, 1} accepts all strings ending with 0.

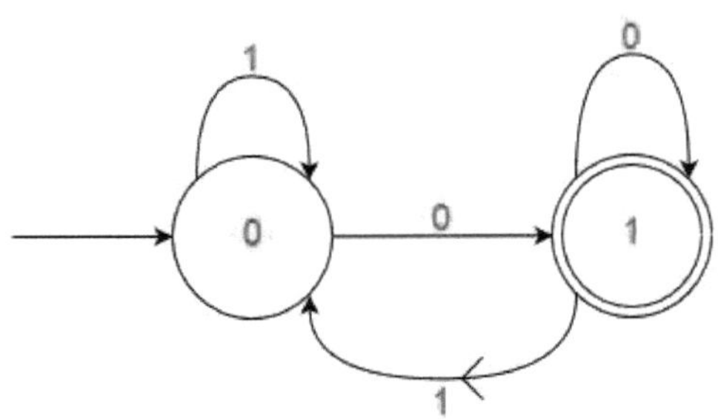

Fig. 2.3 DFA that recognizes all Strings that end with 0

It is possible to construct more than one DFA for a given pattern of strings. But, a DFA with a minimum number of states is generally preferred.

Non-deterministic Finite Automata (NFA):

NFA is similar to DFA with the following additional features:

1. It allows Null (or ε) moves, i.e., it can move forward without reading symbols.

2. It has the ability to change its state to more than one state for a particular input.

However, these additional features don't add any power to NFA. If we compare both in terms of power, both are equivalent. Due to the above additional features, NFA has a different transition function (**δ**), the rest is the same as DFA.

δ: Q X (Σ U ε) --> 2 ^ Q.

In the transition function defined above, we can clearly see that for any input including null (or ε), NFA can go to any state number of states. For example, below is an NFA for the above problem.

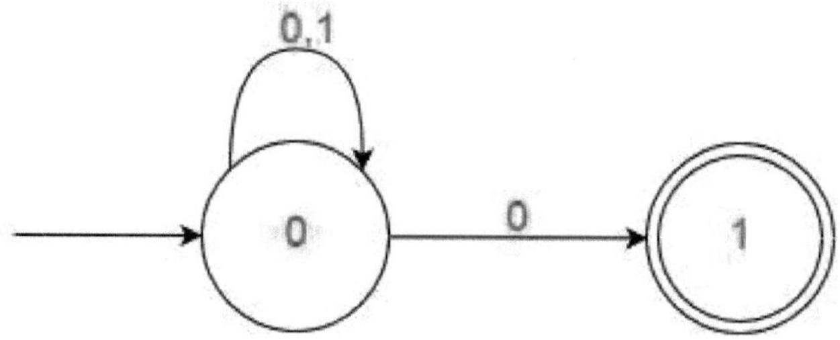

Fig. 2.4 NFA that recognizes all Strings ending with 0

In NFA, if there exists a path for a given input string that leads to a final state (the one represented using double circle), then the input string is considered as accepted. For example, in the above NFA, there are multiple paths for the input string "00". Since one of the paths leads to the final state, "00" is accepted by the above NFA.

DFA Vs. NFA:

Both NFA and DFA have the same power and each NFA can be translated into a DFA. There can be multiple final states in both DFA and NFA.

All the tuples in DFA and NFA are the same except for one, which is Transition Function (δ). In case of DFA δ :

Q X Σ --> Q

and in NFA δ :

Q X Σ --> 2Q

Now if we observe we will be able to find out *Q X Σ –> Q* is part of *Q X Σ –> 2Q.*

On the RHS side, Q is the subset of 2Q which indicates Q is contained in 2Q or Q is a part of 2Q, however, the reverse isn't true. So mathematically, we can conclude that every DFA is NFA but not vice-versa. Yet there is a way to convert an NFA to DFA, so there exists an equivalent DFA for every NFA.

Here is a comparison between NFA and DFA:

1. All transitions are deterministic in DFA (i.e., each transition leads to exactly one state). Whereas, transitions could be non-deterministic in NFA (i.e., a transition could lead to a subset of states)
2. In DFA, at each state, the transition on all possible symbols should be defined. But for NFA, not all symbols necessarily have to be defined for each state.
3. Every DFA is a special case of NFA. For any NFA, N with 'n' states, the corresponding DFA, D can have 2n states.

Other Notataions for Modelling:

Regular Expression (RE) is a structural notation for describing the same pattern that can be represented by a finite automata. RE is used in software such as Operating System (OS) for searching a file name based on some pattern.

Context Free Grammar (CFG) is another structural notation that can be used for describing the structure of a programming languages like C. Using CFG, the parser component of a compiler can be designed.

Turing Machine (TM) is also a computation model that helps us to know the decidability and intractability of an abstract machine. With the help of a Turing Machine, we can identify whether a problem can be computed by a machine like computer. It also lets us distinguish tractable and intractable problems.

CHAPTER THREE

Introduction to Regular Expression

Regular Expression is another language-defining notation. Regular expressions are closely related to Non-Deterministic Finite Automata (NFA) and can be though of as a "user-friendly" alternate to the NFA notation for describing software components. They are capable of defining a language consisting of a set of strings formed using one or more alphabets.

A language is said to be **regular** if it can be expressed in terms of a regular expression. Regular Languages are the most restricted types of languages and are accepted by finite automata.

	Regular Expression	Regular Languages
set of vovels	$(a \cup e \cup i \cup o \cup u)$	{a, e, i, o, u}
a followed by 0 or more b	$(a.b^{*})$	{a, ab, abb, abbb, abbbb,....}
any no. of vowels followed by any no. of consonants	$v^{*}.c^{*}$ (where v – vowels and c – consonants)	{ ε , a ,aou, aiou, b, abcd.....} where ε represent empty string (in case 0 vowels and o consonants)

Fig. 3.1 Regular Expression and the Language defined by it

Here is an example: The language defined by the Regular Expression

$$(0+1)^*0(0+1)^*0(0+1)^*$$

over the alphabet {0,1} is the set of all strings containing at least two 0's.

Regular Expressions:

Deterministic and Non-deterministic Finite Automata are machine-like descriptions of a language, whereas Regular Expressions are algebraic descriptions of a language. Using regular expressions, we can express a language in a declarative way. Hence, regular expressions serve as the input language for many systems that process strings.

For instance, search commands such as grep in UNIX OS use a regular expression like notation for describing patterns that the user wants to find in a file. The following is a simple regular expression that denotes a language consists of all strings having either a single 0 followed by any number of 1's or a single 1 followed by any number of 0's:

01* + 10*

Forming Regular Expressions:

Regular Expressions are algebraic notations used to denote regular languages. Here are some rules for forming a regular expression:

- ϕ is a regular expression for regular language ϕ.
- ε is a regular expression for regular language {ε}.
- If $a \in \Sigma$ (Σ represents the input alphabet), ***a*** is a regular expression with language {a}.
- If ***a*** and ***b*** are regular expression, a + b is also a regular expression with language {a,b}.
- If ***a*** and ***b*** are regular expression, ab (concatenation of a and b) is also regular.
- If ***a*** is regular expression, ***a**** (0 or more times a) is also regular.

Two regular expressions are equivalent if languages generated by them are same. For example, (a+b*)* and (a+b)* generate the same language. Every string which is generated by (a+b*)* is also generated by (a+b)* and vice versa.

Example 1: The regular expression 0*(10*)* and (1*0)*1* are equal. Because the language defined by both of them are same.

Example 2: The following are the regular expressions that define the language on input alphabets a and b, in which two a's do not come together

(b + ab)* + (b +ab)*a

a(b + ba)* + (b + ba)*

The language defined by the Regular Expressions given above is as follows:

L={ε, a, b, bb, ab, aba, ba, bab, baba, abab, ...}

As the language defined by them are same, they are said to be equivalent regular expressions.

Operators used in a Regular Expression

There are three operations that can be used to represent a language denoted by a regular expression. They are:

1. Union of wo languages L and M
2. Concatenation of two languages and
3. Closure (or star, or Kleen Closure) of a language L

Union Operator (U)

The Union of two languages L and M, denoted by LUM, is the set of all strings that are either in L or M, or both. For example,

if L = {001, 10, 111} and
M = {ε, 001} then
LUM = {ε, 001, 10, 111}

Concentation Operator (.)

The Concatenation of languages L and M is the set of all strings that can be formed by taking any string in L and concatenating it with any one of the strings in M. While performing concatenation, one string is followed by the other to form the result of the concatenation.

For example,
if L = {001, 10, 111} and
M = {ε, 001} then
L.M or just LM = {001, 10, 111, 001001, 10001, 111001}

The conctenation operator is denoted using a dot, or no operator at all. In the resultant language, the first three strings of LM are concatenation of strings in L with ε in M. However, the last three strings in LM are formed by taking each string in L and concatenating them with the second string in M, which is 001.

The Closure (*) Operator

The closure (or star, or Kleen Closure) of a language L is denoted by L* and represents the set of those strings that can be formed by taking any no. of strings from L, possibly with repetitions (i.e., the same string may be selected more than once) and concatenating all of them.

For instance, if L={0,1}

then L* is a set of strings formed using any number of 0's and 1's.

Here is another example:

if L={0, 11} the L* consists of those strings of 0's and 1's such that the 1's come in pairs, e.g., 011, 011110, 11110 and ε, but not 01011 or 101.

CHAPTER FOUR

Finite Automata

Finite automata, or finite – state machines are a mathematical way of describing particular kinds of algorithm (or "machines"). In particular, finite automata can be used to describe the process of recognizing patterns in input strings, and so can be used to construct scanners. There is also of course, a strong relationship between finite automata and regular expressions.

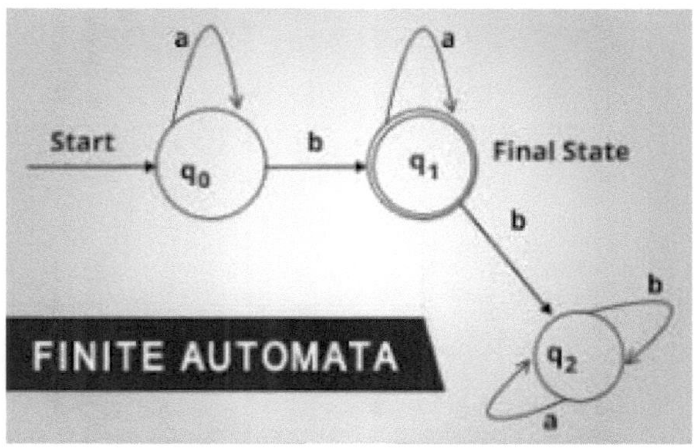

Fig. 4.1 Finite Automata recognizing the Regular Expression a*ba*

A finite automata consists of a finite number of states and a finite number of transitions, and these transitions are defined on certain, specific symbols called input symbol. One of the states of the finite automata is identified as the initial state, the state in which the automata always starts. Similarly, certain states are identified as final states. Therefore, a finite automata is specified as using five things:

1. The states of the finite automata (denoted as Q)
2. The input symbols on which transitions are made (Σ)

3. The transition function (δ) that specifies from which state on which input symbol where the transition goes.
4. The initial state (q_0), and
5. The set of final states (F)

Therefore formally a finite automata is a five tuple expression in the form:

$M = (Q,E,\delta,q_0,F)$

If from a state P there exists a transition going to state q on an input symbol a, then we write.

$\delta(P,a) = q$.

Hence, δ is a function whose domain is a set of ordered pairs of the form (p,a), where p is a state and a is an input symbol, and the range is a set of states. Therfore, δ is considered as a mapping function, which defines a mapping from

$Q \times \Sigma$ to Q

The following is a finite automata which can recognize a language that starts with any binary number (0|1) but ends with a binary number 0. This language can be expressed in a Regular expression as (0|1)*0.

$M = (\{q_0, q_1\}, \{0,1\}, \delta, q_0, \{q_1\})$

Where,

$\delta(q_0, 0) = q_1, \delta(q_0,1) = q_0$

$\delta(q_1, 0) = q_1, \delta(q_1,1) = q_0$

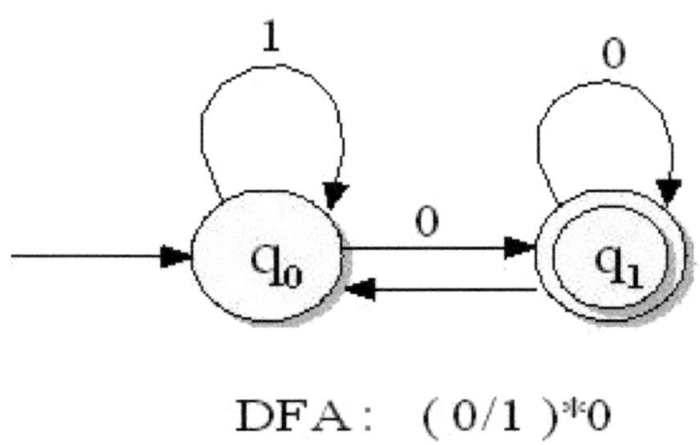

Fig. 4.2 DFA Represenation of the Regular Expression (0|1)*0

A Finite Automata can be represented pictorially in two ways: using graph and using tables. The graphical notation of a finite automata is called a "transition diagram of finite automata".

In a transition diagram the vertices of the graph correspond to the states of the automata, the edges of the graph correspond to the transition that takes place between the initial state and the final state of the automata.

In a tabular representation the table consists of rows and columns. Rows correspond to the states of the diagram and the columns correspond to the input symbols and their transition. The first row specifies the transition from the initial state; the rows specifying the transition from the final states are marked as *.

The automata shown above is the equivalent NFA of the DFA shown in Fig 4.2:

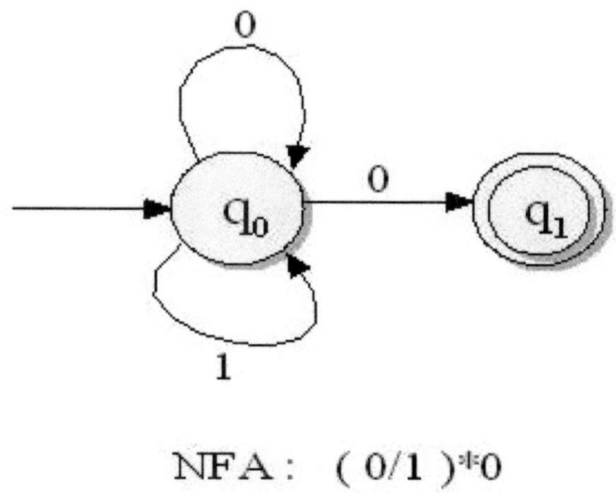

Fig. 4.3 NFA Equivalent of the DFA shown in Fig. 4.2

CHAPTER FIVE

More Design Notations

A grammar is also a modelling notation that makes use of a set of production rules for defining a language consists of stings of various length. It helps us to define a finite set of formal rules for generating syntactically correct and meaningful sentences.

Fig. 5.1 Relation between Regular Grammar and Context Free Grammar

Given a grammar G, its corresponding language L(G) represents the set of all strings generated from G. Consider the following grammar,

G: S-> aSb|ε

In this grammar, using the production

S-> ε,

we can generate ε. Therefore, ε is part of L(G).

Similarly, using the production

S=>aSb=>ab, ab is generated. Similarly, aabb can also be generated.

Here is another grammar that defines a set of strings formed using a sequence of a's followed by squence of b's. It also denotes an empty sting - a string with out a or b.

$$L(G) = \{a^n b^n, n>=0\}$$

$$L(G) = \{\varepsilon, ab, aabb, aaabbb, \dots \}$$

In the language L(G) discussed above, the condition n = 0 is taken to accept ε. When n>=1, the number of a's and number of b's present in the string of L(G) are equal.

Key Points about Grammar and the Language defined by it:

1. For a given grammar G, its corresponding language L(G) is unique.
2. The language L(G) corresponding to grammar G must contain all strings which can be generated from G.
3. The language L(G) corresponding to grammar G must not contain any string which can not be generated from G.

Context-Free Grammar

Grammar is basically composed of two basic elements - Terminals and Non-terminals.

Terminal Symbols: Terminal symbols are those which are the components of the sentences generated using a grammar and are represented using small case letter like a, b, c etc.

Non-Terminal Symbols: Non-Terminal Symbols are those symbols which take part in the generation of the sentence but are not the component of the sentence. Non-Terminal Symbols are also called Auxiliary Symbols or Variables. These symbols are represented using a capital letter like A, B, C, etc.

Formal Definition of Grammar

Any Grammar can be represented by 4 tuples – <N, T, P, S>

N – Finite Non-Empty Set of Non-Terminal Symbols.

T – Finite Set of Terminal Symbols.

P – Finite Non-Empty Set of Production Rules.

S – Start Symbol (Symbol from where we start producing our sentences or strings).

Production Rules: A production or production rule is a statement specifying a symbol substitution that can be recursively performed to generate new symbol sequences. It is of the form α-> β where α is a Non-Terminal Symbol which can be replaced by β which is a string of Terminal Symbols or Non-Terminal Symbols.

A **Context Free Grammar** (CFG) is a way of describing languages by recursive rules called productions. A CFG consists of a set of variables, a set of terminals symbols, and a start variable as well as the productions. Each production consists of a head variable and a body consisting of a string of zero, or more variables and/or terminals.

Example-1:

Consider Grammar G1 = <N, T, P, S>

Where,

T = {a,b} is a aet of terminal symbols

P = {A->Aa, A->Ab, A->a, A->b, A->ε } is a set of all production rules

S = {A} denotes the Start Symbol

As the start symbol is S then we can produce Aa, Ab, a, b, which can further produce strings by replacing A with terminals - a or b, and hence this grammar can be used to produce strings of the form (a+b)*.

Example-2:

S -> aSa|bSb|a|b

The language generated by the above grammar over the alphabet {a,b} is the set of odd length palindromes. Using S->a and S->b, a and b can be generated. Similarly using S=>aSa=>aba, aba can be generated. Other strings which can be generated from grammar are: a, b, aba, bab, aaa, bbb, ababa, ...

Turing Machine

A Turing Machine (TM) is a kind of state machine, which is much more powerful than Finite Automata (FA) and Push Down Automata (PDA). It is a mathematical model that consists of the following three elements:

1. An infinite length tape divided into cells on which input symbols are stored for acceptance or processing.
2. A Read Write (RW) Head that can move one position right or left at a time to read one symbol at a time from the tape.
3. A Control unit that has control over the states of the Turing Machine to decide when a state transition may occur depending on the current input symbol read from the tape.

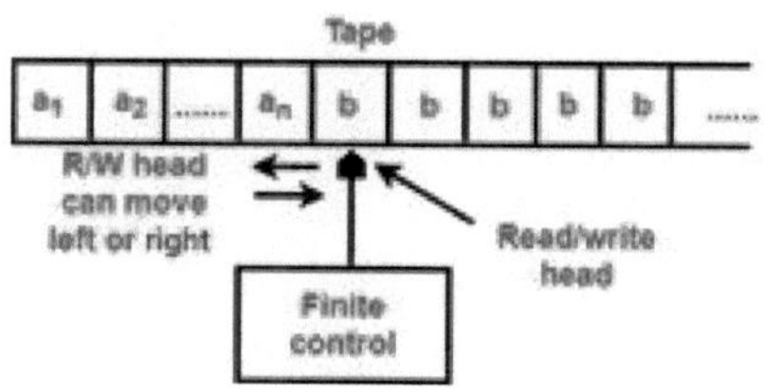

Fig. 5.2 Three Basic Elements of a Turing Machine

The tape is divided into a sequence of numbered cells. Each cell can contain a symbol and cells that don't contain an input symbol are assumed to have a blank symbol (B). The set of symbols of the tape is denoted by T.

In a single step, a tape head reads the contents of a cell on the tape (reads a symbol), replaces it with some other character (writes a symbol) and reposition itself to right or left one position of the current cell or doen't move at all.

The control unit determines the reading and writing activity of the RW Head. It determines when the RW Head has to move and when it should read or write from the tape. It also has the control over the various states of the Turing Machine. The varous states represented in a Turing Machine include the following:

- Intitial State (q0)
- Halt State h (one or more)
- Other States that stands between initial and the halt state.

SECTION II - Compiler Design

CHAPTER SIX

Introduction to Compilers

A translator is a system software that takes as input - code written in one programming language (source code) and produces as output - code in another language (target program).

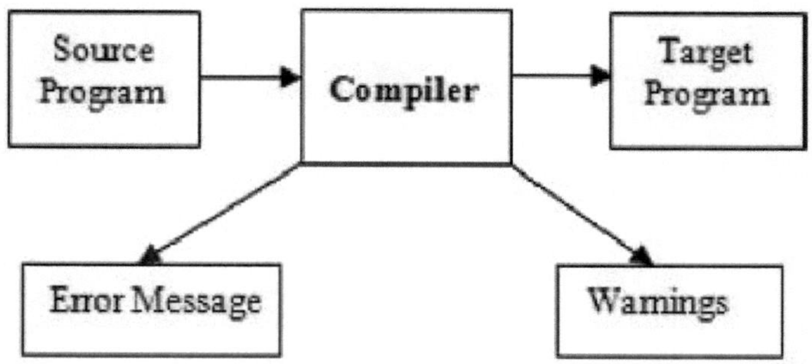

Fig. 6.1 The Role of a Compiler

A **compiler** is a program that reads a program written in one language - the **source language** and translates it into an equivalent program in another language – the **target language**. During this process, the compiler reports to its user the presence of errors in the source program.

The role of a compiler is to process a program written in a High Level Language (HLL) and to convert it into an object program (also called targe program). The resulting object program will be loaded into memory for execution.

If the source code is written using one of the high level languages such as FORTRAN, PL/1 or COBOL and the object code is to be generated in Low Level Language such as Assembly Language or machine language, then the translator used for translation is called a **Compiler**.

Need for Translators:

Using machine language, programmers communicate directly with the computer in terms of bits, registers and primitive machine operations. The instructions are given in the form of 0's and 1's. This makes programming a tedious and time consuming task when the complexity of the algorithm is increased.

Moreover, all operations and operands are specified using numeric code and hence the programs written in machine language are cryptic. This makes the code very difficult to modify in a convenient manner. Therefore, to make coding simpler and easier, the following system software were introduced:

Interpreter: Interpreter is a translator that transforms a source program written in a high level language or an intermediary code (byte code in Java) into a code executed by the machine. In some cases, the source code itself can be considered as the intermediate code. In that case, the interpreter translates the statements written in the source code line by line.

Interpreters are often less complex than that of compilers and facilitate some of the complex programming language constructs. However, the main disadvantage of interpreter is that the execution time of an interpreted program is usually slow than that of a corresponding compiled object program.

Preprocessor: Preprocessors are one kind of translator that take as input code written in one high level language and produce the equivalent code in the same language or in another high level language. For example, there are many FORTRAN preprocessors that map 'structured' versions of FORTRAN into conventional FORTRAN.

Assembler: An assembler is a translator, which takes an assembly language program as input and converts it into a machine language program.

Assesmbly Vs. High Level Languages:

In assembly language, we use mnemonic names for both operation codes and data addresses. For example,

ADD X,Y

is an assembly language instruction for adding the content of X and Y registers. Such programs are easier to write and understand than machine language programs. Because, numeric codes for addresses and operations (in machine language) are replaced with more meaningful symbolic codes.

A computer however, can't execute a program written using an assembly language. Assembly language programs have to be translated to machine language, using an Assembler. The major drawback of writing programs in assembly language is that the programmer must be intimately concerned with how and where data is represented within the machine.

A High-Level programming language on the other hand allows a programmer to express algorithms in a more natural notation. For example "A+B" is an expression in a high-level language that instructs a computer to add the contents of variables A and B.

COBOL, FORTRAN, PL/1, ALGOL, SNOBOL, APL, PASCAL, LISP and C are some of the more common high-level languages. A high-level language makes the programming task simpler, but requires a program to translate its code to the corresponding machine code for its execution.

Language Processing System

The following figure shows the various programs involved in a language – processing system:

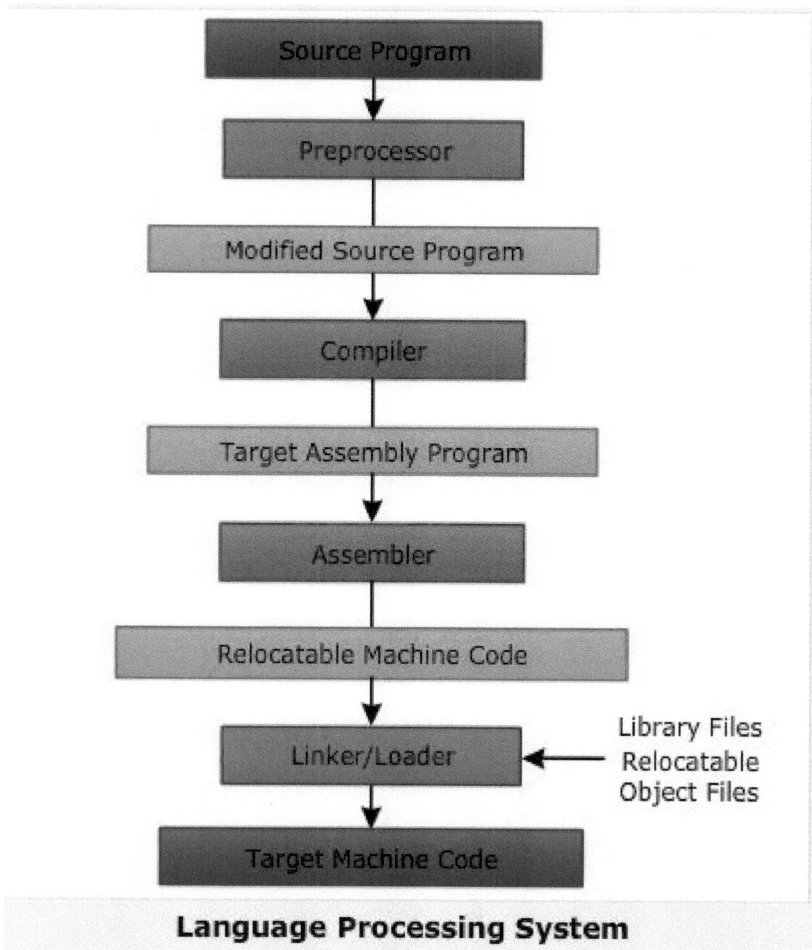

Fig. 6.2 Steps involved in a language processing system

A source program may be divided into modules stored in separate files. To compile and build executables of such programs, we need several programs, which include a compiler, a preprocessor, an assembler and a loader / linkage editor.

The task of collecting the source program is sometimes entrusted to a special program called preprocessor. The preprocessor may also expand short hands, called macros, into source language statements.

The target program created by the compiler may require further processing before it can be run. The compiler usually creates assembly code that is translated by an assembler into machine code, which is then linked together with, some library routines into the code that actually runs on the machine.

CHAPTER SEVEN

Phases of a Compiler

A compiler takes as input a source program and produces as output an equivalent sequence of machine instructions. This process of compilation is so complex, that it can't be performed in single step. For this reason, the entire process of compilation is partitioned into a series of sub processes called phases, each of which transforms the source program from one representation to another.

A typical decomposition of a compiler is shown in the below figure.

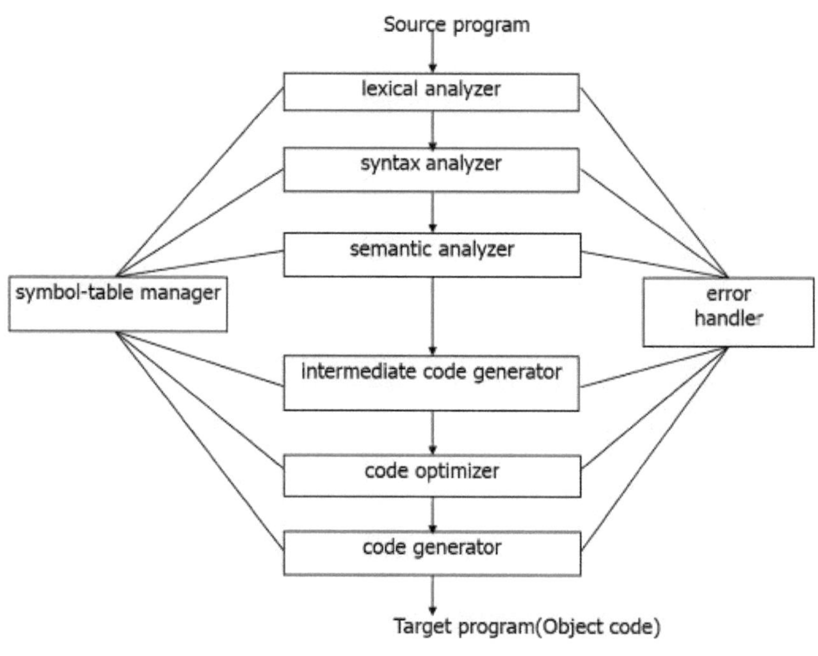

Fig. 6.1 Six Phases of a Compiler

A **phase** is a logically cohesive operation that takes as input one representation of the source program and produces as output another representation. There are six different phases of operations performed while converting a high level language program into a machine language equivalent in a compiler.

The first three phases, forming the bulk of the **analysis** portion of a compiler, and the remaining phases forms the **synthesis** part of the compiler. The two activities symbol table management and error handling interact with almost all phases of compilation.

Lexical Analyzer:

This is the first phase of a compiler, in which each and every character of the source program is separated and grouped into meaningful symbols called **tokens.** The usual tokens are: **keywords** such as *Do* or *IF*, **identifiers** such as *X* or *NUM*, **operator symbols** such as <= or + and **punctuation symbols** such as *parenthesis* or *commas*. Each and every token is identified by a code which we may regard as integers. Thus, *Do* might be represented by 1, + by 2, and *identifier* by 3.

Syntax Analyzer:

The syntax analyzer groups tokens together into syntactic structures. For example, the three tokens representing *A*, + and *B* might be grouped into a syntactic structure like A+B, which is an expression. Often the syntactic structure of a statement is organized as a tree whose leaves are tokens. The interior nodes of the tree represent strings of tokens that logically belong to each other.**Intermediate Code Generator :**

This phase uses the structure provided by the syntax analyzer to create a stream of simple instructions. Many styles of intermediate code are possible. One common style uses instructions with one operator and a small number of operands. For example, the syntactic structure *A+B* may be written using a sequence of simple instructions as given below:

LOAD B
LOAD A
STORE B

The primary difference between intermediate code and assembly code is that the intermediate code need not specify the registers to be used for each operation.

Code Optimizer:

This is an optional phase, that can be used to improve the intermediate code. Its output is another intermediate code that does the same job as the original, but perhaps in a way that saves time and/or space.

Code Generation:

This phase performs the conversion of intermediate code into object code that could be understood by the machine. This code is actually produced by deciding on the memory locations for data, selecting code to access each datum and selecting the registers in which each computation is to be done.

Table Management & Error Handling:

These are the two more phases (sub tasks) of a compiler, using which tasks such as book keeping and error handling are performed. A table is used by the compiler to keep track of the names used by the program. Through error handling, faults in the source program are identified and informed to the user in each and every phase. Both table management and error handling routines interact with all other phases of compiler.

CHAPTER EIGHT

Types of Compiler

Compilers are often classified as **single-pass**, **multi-pass**, **load-and-go**, **debugging or optimizing**, depending on how they have been constructed or what function they are supposed to perform.

In an implementation of a compiler, portions of one or more phases are combined into a module called a **pass.** A **pass** reads the source program or the output of the previous pass, makes the transformation specified by its passes, and writes output into an intermediate file, which may then be read by a subsequent pass.

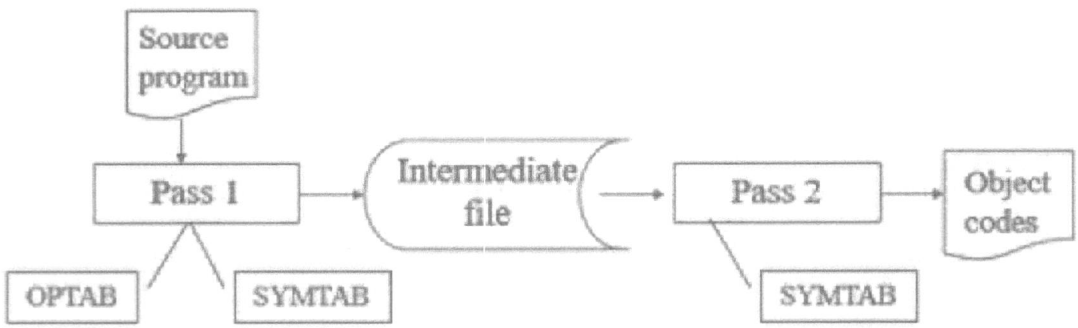

Fig. 8.1 Two Pass Assember/Compiler

The number of passes and the grouping of phases into passes are usually determined based on many criteria such as follows:

i. The structure of the source language
ii. The environment (machine) in which the compiler must operate

Certain languages require at least two passes to generate code easily. For example, languages such as PL/1 or ALGOL 68 allow the declaration of a name to occur after the usage of that name. In such scenario, code for expressions containing the name can't be generated conveniently until the declaration has been seen.

Pascal and C are both languages that permit one-pass compilation. In **one pass compiler**, all phases occur during a single pass. This results in efficient compilation but also in less efficient target code.

Need for Multi-Pass Compiler:

A multi-pass compiler can be made to use in a computer with small memory, because it makes use of less space for its compilation than that of the single pass compiler. But, it is slower in speed, because each pass reads and writes an intermediate file. Thus, compilers running on a computer with **small memory** would normally use several passes, while, on a computer with larger memory, a compiler with fewer passes would be possible.

Compiler with **optimization** often use more than one pass; a typical arrangement is one pass for scanning and parsing, one pass for semantic analysis and source-level optimization, and a third pass for code generation and target level optimization.

Reducing Number of Passes in a Compiler:

Each pass in a compiler is a transformation process that transforms a stream of data into an intermediate form of the source program. A phase takes as input one representation of the source code and produces as output another representation. The intermediate representation of the source code are stored in storage structures like array that can be given as input to the following phases.

The reading and writing of intermediate files is a time consuming job, which affects the efficiency of the compiler. In order to overcome this difficulty several phases are combined into one pass so that the operation of the phases may be interleaved, with control alternating. This integration of phases into one or more passes can be achieved using a technique called **back patching.**

Back Packing:

In back patching, if the output of a phase can't be determined without looking at the remainder of the phase's input, the phase will generate output with "slots", which can be filled in later, after more of the input is read. For example an assembler might have a statement like:

GOTO L

which precedes a statement with labels L.

A two pass assembler uses its first pass to enter its symbol table a list of all identifiers (statement labels and data names) together with the machine address (relative to the beginning of the program) to which these identifiers correspond. Then a second pass replaces mnemonic operation codes, such as GOTO, by their machine language equivalent and replaces uses of identifiers by their machine address.

A one-pass assembler, on the other hand, could generate a skeleton of the GOTO machine instruction the first time it saw GOTO L. It could then append the machine address for this instruction once the machine address for L is determined. For example, when the assembly encounters a statement such as

L: ADD X

it scans a list of statements referring to L and places the machine address of statement *L : ADD X* in the address field of each such instruction. Subsequent assembly instructions referring to L can have the value for L substituted immediately.

The distance over which back patching occurs is important since the code to be back patched must remain accessible until back patching is complete. In a compiler, most of the back patching is done over relatively short distances. In languages like ALGOL, where each program is written as a single procedure, back patching is not possible due to forward jumps that may traverse the active length of the program.

CHAPTER NINE

Analysis Synthesis Model of Compilation

There are two parts in compilation – Analysis and Synthesis. The **analysis** part breaks up the source program into constituent pieces and creates an intermediate representation of the source program. The **synthesis** part constructs the designated target program from the intermediate representation of the source program. Among the two parts, synthesis requires the most specialized techniques.

During analysis, the operations implied by the source program are determined and recorded in a hierarchical structure called **tree**. Often, a special kind of tree called a **syntax tree** is used, in which each node represents an operation and the children of a node represent the arguments of the operation. A syntax tree for an assignment statement is shown in the below figure:

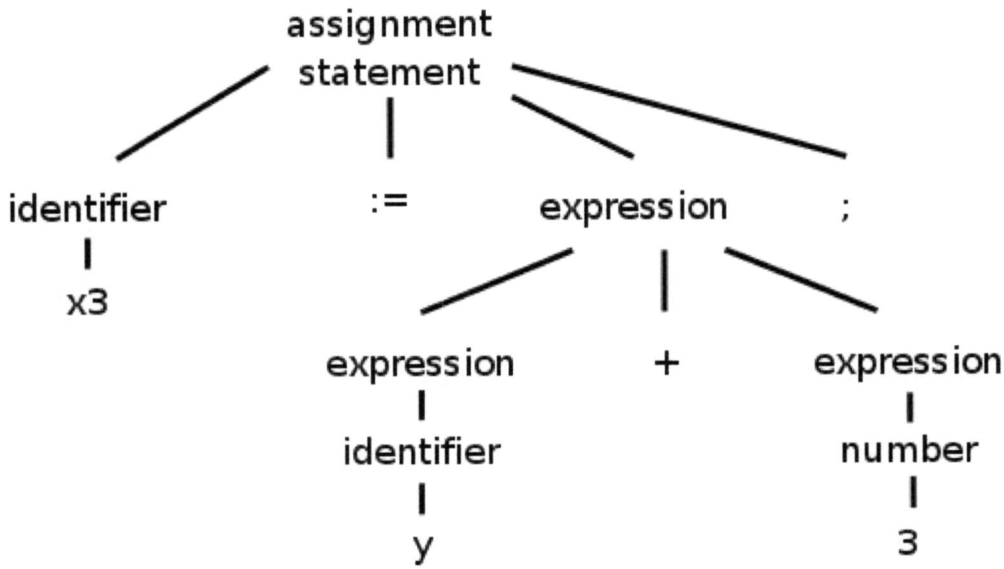

Fig. 9.1 Syntax Tree of an Assignment Statement

Three Phases of Analysis Part of a Compiler

In compiling, analysis consists of three phases :

1. Linear analysis
2. Hierarchical analysis
3. Semantic analysis

In Linear analysis, the stream of characters making up the source program is read from left-to-right and grouped into tokens, which are sequences of characters having a collective meaning.

In hierarchical analysis, tokens are grouped hierarchically into nested collections with collective meaning. And in semantic analysis, certain checks are performed to ensure that the components of a program fit together meaningfully.

Lexical or Linear Analysis:

In a compiler, the linear analysis is sometimes called as lexical analysis or scanning. For example in lexical analysis the characters in the assignment statement:

position := initial + rate * 60

would be grouped into the following:

1. The identifier - position
2. The assignment symbol - :=
3. The identifier - initial
4. The plus sign - +
5. The identifier - rate
6. The multiplication sign - *
7. The number - 60

The blanks separating the characters of these tokens would normally be eliminated during lexical analysis.

Syntax Analysis:

The Hierarchical analysis of a compiler is also called as parsing or syntax analysis. It involves grouping the tokens of the source program into grammatical phrases that are to be used by the compiler to synthesize output. Usually, the grammatical phrases of the source program are represented by a parse tree such as the one shown below:

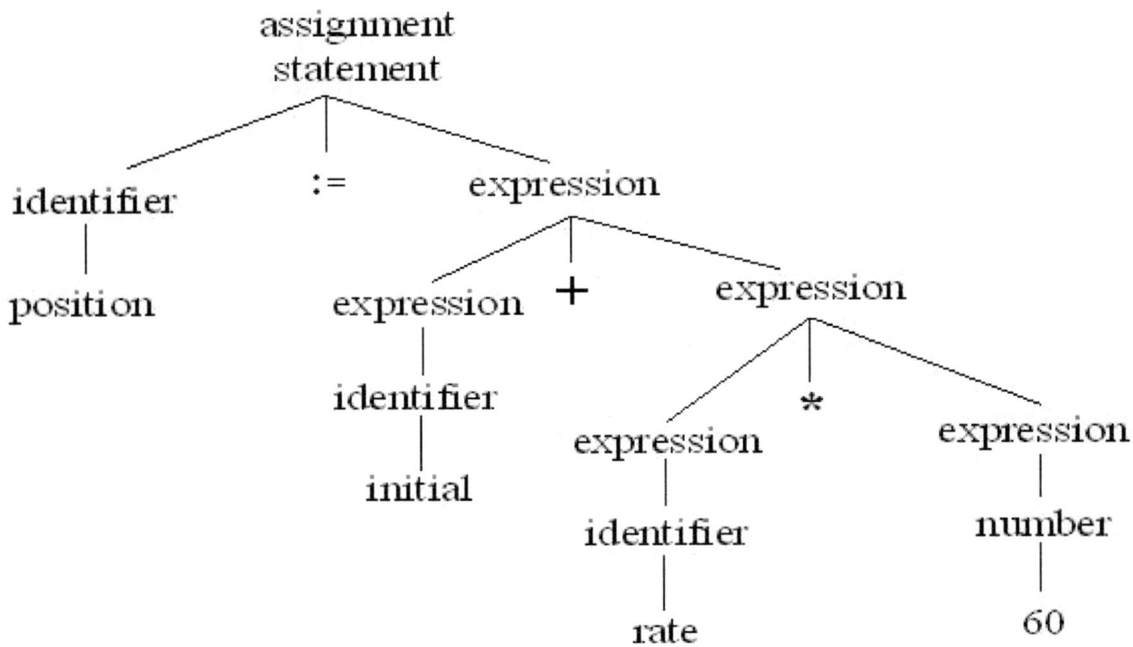

Fig. 9.2 Parse Tree Constructed for an Assignment Statement

The hierarchical structure of a program is usually expressed using recursive rules. For example we might have the following rules as part of the definition of expressions:

1. Any identifier is an expression
2. Any number is an expression
3. If expression1 and expression2 are expressions then the following are also valid expressions:

   expression1 + expression2
   expression1 * expression2
   (expression1)

In this definition, Rules (1) and (2) are (non recursive) basic rules, while (3) defines expressions in terms of operators applied to other expressions. Thus, by rule (1), ***initial*** and ***rate*** are expressions. By rule (2) ***60*** is an expression, while by rule (3), we can first infer that ***rate*60*** is an expression, and finally that

initial + ***rate* 60***

is also an expression.

The parse tree, which is generated as the output from syntax analysis phase describes the syntactic structure of the input. But a more common internal representation of the syntactical structure is shown in a syntax tree given below:

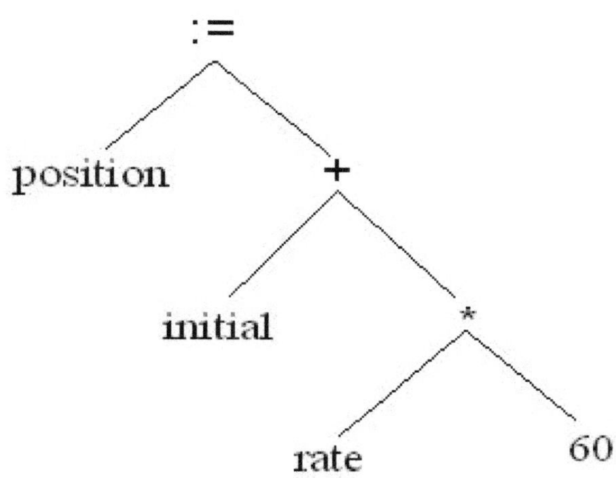

Fig. 9.2 Syntax Tree for an Assignment Statement

A syntax tree is a compressed representation of the parse tree in which the operations appear as the interior nodes, and the operands are represented using child nodes of the node containing the operator.

Semantic Analysis:

The semantic analysis phase checks the source program for semantic errors and gather type information for the subsequent code generation phase. It uses the hierarchical structure determined by the syntax analysis phase to identify the operators and operands of expressions and statements.

An important component of semantic analysis is type checking. Here, the compiler checks that each operator has operands that are permitted by the source language specification.

CHAPTER TEN

Lexical Analysis

The lexical analysis phase reads the characters from the source program and groups them into a stream of tokens, in which each token represents a logically cohesive sequence of characters, such as an identifier, a keyword (if, while, etc.), a punctuation character, or a multi character operator like :=. The character sequence forming a token is called the **lexeme** for the token.

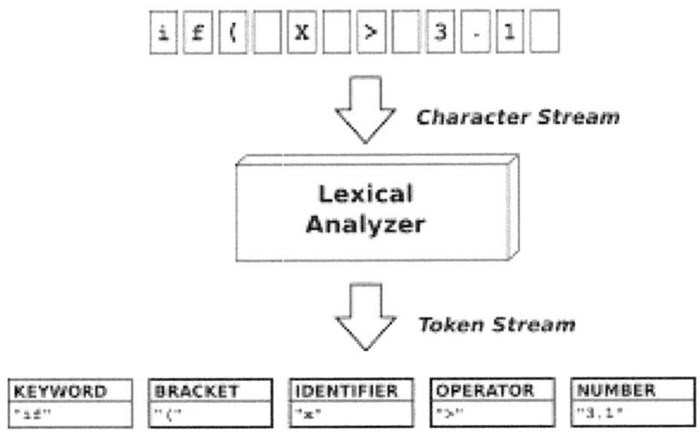

Fig. 10.1 Role of a Lexical Analyzer

Certain tokens will be augmented by a “lexical value”. For example, when an identifier like *rate* is found, the lexical analyzer not only generates a token, say ID, but also enters the lexeme - *rate* into the symbol table, if it is not already there. The lexical value associated with this occurrence of ID points to the symbol table entry for rate.

Tokens fall into several categories. They include the reserved words, such as IF and THEN, special symbol such as ‘+’ and ‘-‘, tokens that represent multiple strings such as NUM and ID, which represent numbers and identifiers.

It is the task of the scanner, a part of the compiler, to read characters from the source code and form them into tokens. Although the scanner converts the entire source program into a sequence of tokens, it will not do this all at once. Instead the scanner will operate under the control of the parser, returning the single next token from the input on demand.

Some of the functions of a lexical analyzer are as follows:

i. Removing the white spaces and comments.
ii. Identifying the constants.
iii. Recognizing identifiers and keywords.

Removing White Spaces and Comments:

Many languages allow "white spaces" (blank spaces, tab spaces, and newlines) to appear between tokens. Such white spaces must be removed before compilation. Comments can likewise be ignored by the parser and code generator, because they are also treated as white spaces. If white spaces and comments are eliminated by the lexical analyzer, the parser will never have to consider them.

Identifying the Constants:

Since an integer constant is a sequence of digits, integer constants are allowed by adding productions to the grammar of expressions, or by creating a token for such constants. Let NUM be the token representing an integer. When a sequence of digits appear in the input stream, the lexical analyzer will pass NUM to the parser. The value of the integer will be parsed along as an attribute of the token - NUM.

Recognizing Identifiers and Keywords:

Languages use identifiers as names of variables, arrays, functions and the like. A grammar for a language often treats an identifier as a token. For example the input

count = count + increment;

would be converted by the lexical analyzer into the token stream

id = id + id;

This token stream is used for parsing. In order to distinguish one instance of **id** from the other, lexeme such as *count* and *increment* are associated with instances of **id**. The lexeme is stored in the symbol table and a pointer to this symbol-table entry becomes an attribute of the token **id**.

Many languages use fixed character strings such as *begin*, *end*, *if* and so on, as punctuation mark or to identify certain constructs. These character strings called **keywords**, generally satisfies the rules for forming identifiers, so a mechanism is needed for deciding when a lexeme forms a keyword and when it forms an identifier.

Interface to the Lexical Analyzer:

When a lexical analyzer is inserted between the parser and the input stream, it interacts with the two in the manner shown in the below figure:

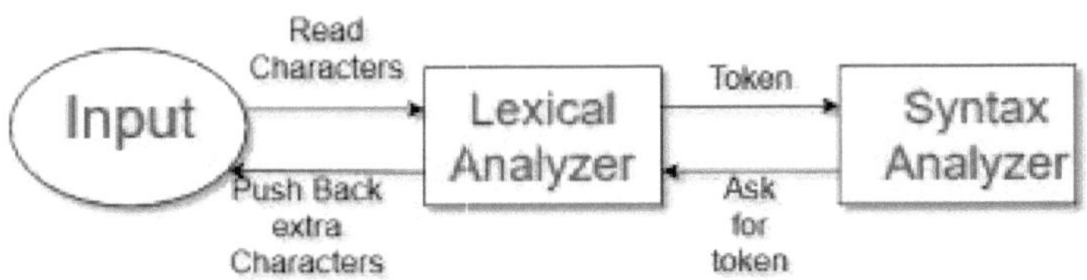

Fig. 10.2 Context of a Lexical Analyzer

The lexical analyzer reads characters from the input, groups them into lexemes, and parses the tokens formed by the lexemes, together with their attribute values, to the later stages of the compiler. In some situations, the lexical analyzer has to read some characters ahead before it can decide on the token to be returned to the parser.

The lexical analyzer and the parser form a producer – consumer pair. The lexical analyzer produces tokens and the parser consumes them. Produced tokens can be held in a token buffer until they are consumed. Commonly, the buffer holds just one token. In this way, the interaction can be implemented simply by making the lexical analyzer a producer called by the parser, returning tokens on demand.

The implementation of reading and pushing back characters is usually done by setting up an input buffer. A block of characters is read into the buffer at a time; a pointer keeps track of the portion of the input that has been analyzed. Pushing back a character is implemented by moving back the pointer.

Need for Lexical Analysis:

The function of the lexical analyzer is to read the source program one character at a time, and to translate it into a sequences of primitive units called tokens. Keywords, identifiers, constants and operators are examples of tokens. The purpose of splitting the analysis of the source program into two phases, lexical analysis and syntax analysis, is to simplify the overall design of the compiler.

It is easier to specify the structure of tokens than the syntactic structure of the source program. Consequently, we can construct a more specialized, and hence more efficient recognizer for tokens than for syntactic structures.

By including certain constructs in the lexical rather than in the syntactic structure, we can greatly simplify the design of the syntax analyzer. For example, a parser embodying the conventions for comments and write spaces is significantly more complex than the one that can assume that comments and white spaces have already been removed by a lexical analyzer.

Steps involved in Designing a Lexical Analyzer:

The steps involved in designing a lexical analyzer are as follows:

1. Select a notation for describing the possible tokens that can appear in the input stream. A notation, such as Regular expression, can be used to describe essentially all the tokens of a programming language.
2. Choose a mechanism to recognize the tokens in the input stream. Examples of such mechanisms used for recognizing tokens are Finite Automata and Transition Diagrams.

Use some mechanisms to perform various actions as the tokens are recognized. For example, an action might enter the value of the token into a table, generate some output, or produce a diagnostic message.

A Simple Approach to the Design of Lexical Analyzer:

The simples approach in designing a lexical analyzer is to describe the behavior of the analyzer using a transition diagram. Transition diagram is a special kind of flowchart, which will remember the previous characters by the position in the flowchart.

In a transition diagram, the boxes of the flowchart are drawn as circles and are called states. The states are connected by arrows, called edges. The labels on the various edges indicate the input characters that can appear after that state. The following is a transition diagram for an identifier, designed to be a letter followed by any number of letters or digits:

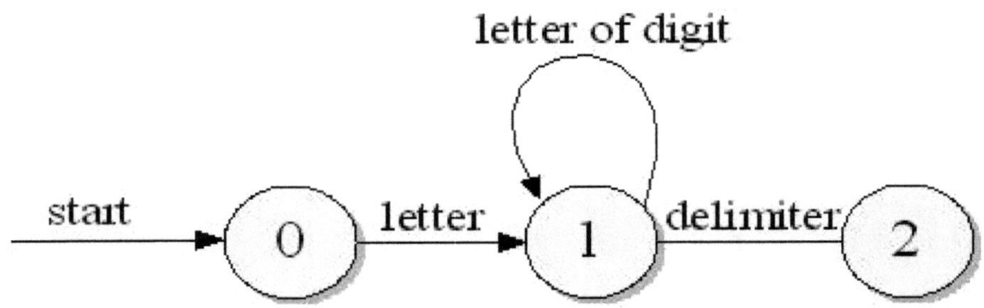

Fig. 10.3 A Transition Diagram for Identifers

In the above figure, the state 0 is the starting state, the edge from which indicates that the first input character must be a letter. If this is the case, we enter state 1 and look at the next input character. If that is a letter on digit, we re – enter state 1 and continue reading letters and digits until the next input character is a delimiter for an identifier. On reading the delimiters, use enter state 2, which is the final one.

CHAPTER ELEVEN

Use of Regular Expression in a Compiler

Regular expression is a notation used for representing or describing the tokens defined for a programming language. Regular expressions represent patterns of strings of characters. A pattern is a rule (format) describing a set of lexemes that can be recognized for producing a partial token by the scanner.

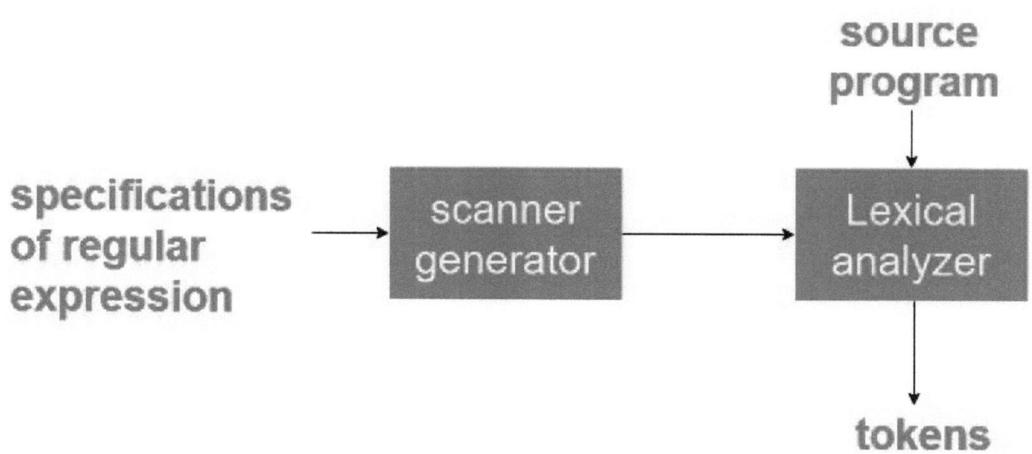

Fig. 11.1 Use of Regular Expression in a Lexical Analyzer

In general, there is a set of strings in the input for which the same token is produced as output. This set of strings is described by a rule called **pattern** which is associated with the token. The pattern is said to match in the set. A **lexeme** is a sequence of characters in the source program that is matched by the pattern for a token. For example, in the Pascal statement

const pi = 1416;

the substring *pi* is a lexeme for the token "identifier".

In most programming languages, the following constructs are treated as tokens: *keywords, operators, identifiers, constants, internal strings and punctuation symbols such as parenthesis, commas and semicolons.* In the example above, when the character sequence *pi* appears in the source program, a token representing an identifier is returned to the parser.

Basics of regular expression:

A regular expression **r** is completely defined by a set of strings that matches. This set is called the language generated by the regular expression and is written as **L(r)**. This language depends, first on the character set that is available. Generally, this will be the set of ASCII characters or some subset of it.

Sometimes the set will be more general than the ASCII character set, in which case the set elements are referred to as symbols. This set of legal symbols is called the **alphabet** and is usually written as the Greek symbol **Σ** (sigma).

A regular expression **r** will also contain characters from the alphabet, but such characters have a different meaning. In a regular expression, all symbols indicate patterns. In addition, a regular expression **r** may contain characters that have special meanings. Such characters are called meta characters or meta symbols.

To describe the meaning of regular expressions and to identify the languages generated by each pattern, we need to know the following basics of regular expressions:

1. Basic Regular Expressions and
2. Regular Expression Operations that generate new regular expressions from existing ones.

Basic Regular Expressions:

These are just the single characters from the alphabet, which match themselves. Given any character **a** from the alphabet Σ, we indicate that the regular expression **a** matches the character *a* by writing

L(a) = {a}.

There are two additional symbols that we will need in special situations: **empty string** and **empty set**. We use the symbol ε (epsilon) to denote the empty string, and the symbol **Ø** for representing the empty set. These additional symbols are defined in a language as follows:

$L(\varepsilon) = \{\varepsilon\}$ and

$L(\emptyset) = \{\ \}$

The difference between these two sets is that the set { } contains no strings at all, while the set { ε } contains the single string consisting of no characters.

Regular Expression Operations:

There are three basic operations in regular expressions:

i. Choice among alternatives, which is indicated by the meta character (|) – Vertical bar.
ii. Concatenation, which is indicated by juxtaposition (without a meta characters); and
iii. Repetition or "closure", which is indicated by the meta character (*).

Choice among alternatives:

If **r** and **s** are regular expressions, then **r|s** is a regular expression which matches any string that is matched either expression **r** or by **s**.

Concatenation:

The concatenation of the regular expressions **r** and **s** is written as **rs**, and it matches any string that is concatenation of two strings, the first of which matches **r** and the second of which matches **s**. For example, the regular expression **ab** matches only the string *ab*, while the expression **(a|b)c** matches the string *ac* and *bc*. The concatenation operation can be written in a regular expression as follows.

L(rs) = L(r) L(s)

Therefore, the above expression (a|b)c can be written in a language notations as:

L((a|b)c) = L(a|b) L(c)

= {a,b} {c}

= {ac,bc}

Repetition:

The repetition operation of a regular expression, sometimes also called Kleene closure, is written $\mathbf{r}^*$, where **r** is a regular expression. The regular expression $\mathbf{r}^*$ matches any finite concatenation of strings, each of which matches **r**. For example $\mathbf{a}^*$ matches the strings

ε, a, aa, aaa, aaaa, ...

Now consider the regular expression $\mathbf{(a|bb)}^*$. This regular expression matches any of the following strings:

ε, a, bb, aa, abb, bba, aaa, aabb and so on.

In terms of languages,

$L((a|bb)^*) = L(a|bb)^*$
$= \{a, bb\}^*$
$= \{\varepsilon, a, bb, aa, ab, bba, bbbb, aaa, aabb, abbbb, \ldots\}$.

Names for Regular Expressions:

Often, it is helpful to give a name to a long regular expression so that we do not have to write the expression itself each time we wish to use it. As an example, if we want to develop a regular expression for a sequence of one or more numeric digits, then we could write

(0|1|2|.....|9)(0|1|2|...|9)*
or we could write
digit digit*
where,
digit = 0|1|2|...|9
is a regular definition of the name digit.

Example:

The regular expression for representing the set of pascal identifiers is as follows:

Letter = A|B|...|Z|a|b|...|z
Digit = 0|1|2|...|9
Id = letter (letter|digit)*
A pascal identifier is a string formed using letters and digits that beginning with a letter.

Precedence Rule

Regular expressions can be formed with parenthesis whenever possible. Parenthesis can be eliminated if we follow the precedence rule while evaluating a regular expression. The following are order of precedence defined in the precedence rule:

* has the highest precedence
. has the next highest precedence
| has the lowest precedence.

Rules for forming Regular Expression:

Each regular expression denotes a language and the regular expressions over alphabet Σ are exactly those expressions that can be constructed from the following rules:

1. ε is a regular expression denoting { ε }, that is the language containing only the empty string.
2. For each **a** in Σ, **a** is a regular expression denoting { a }, the language with only one string, that string consisting of the symbol a.
3. If **R** and **S** are regular expressions denoting languages L_R and L_S, respectively, then:

i. **(R)|(S)** is a regular expression denoting L_R U L_S.
ii. **(R).(S)** is a regular expression denoting L_R. L_S
iii. **(R)*** is a regular expression denoting L_R*

The regular expression a denotes {a}, which is different from just the string a. it should be clear from context whether we are talking about a as a regular expression on as a string.

Examples of Regular Expressions:

The regular expression a* denotes the closure of the language {a}, ie, a* = U {a^i}. Here, the Regular expression a* denotes the set of all strings of zero or more a's.

The regular expression aa* is parsed as a(a)*, and denotes the string of one or more a's.

The expression a|ba* is grouped a|(b(a)*) and denotes the set of strings consisting of either a single a or a b followed by zero of more a's.

The regular expression (aa|ab|ba|bb)* denotes all strings of even length. ε is also a string of even length, zero.

What does the regular expression (a|b) denote?*

The regular expression (a|b) denotes the language {a,b}

Thus (a|b)* denotes U $\{a,b\}^i$

which is the set of all strings of a's and b's, including the empty string.

Recognizer:

Recognizer is a part of a lexical analyzer that identifies the presence of a token on the input. It is a program that takes as input a string x and answers "yes" if x is a sentence if the language L and "no" otherwise.

CHAPTER TWELVE

Constructing NFA and DFA

A Non – Deterministic Finite Automata is a finite automata in which there may exist more than one path corresponding to * in Σ*. In a NDFA, zero or more transitions are permitted from a state on an input symbol.

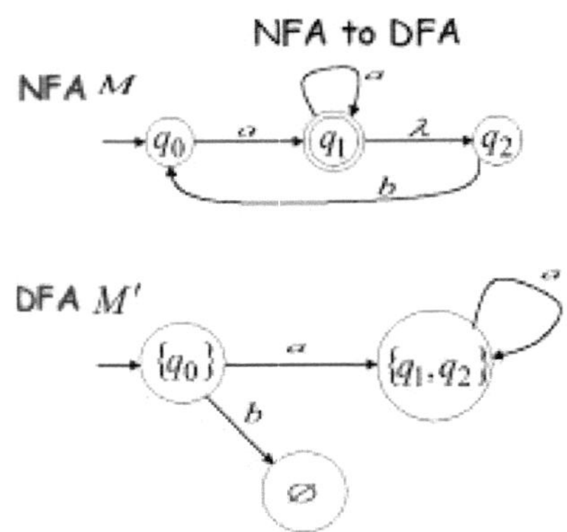

Fig. 12.1 NFA and Its Corresponding DFA

It is easy to convert a regular expression to a non–deterministic finite automata (NDFA). This conversion can be done by representing the regular expression in a generalized transition diagram. This diagram is also called as non-deterministic finite automata.

A NDFA is a labeled directed graph. The nodes are called states, and the labeled edges are called transitions. Generally, a NFA looks almost like a transition diagram, but edges can be labeled by ε as well as characters, and the same character can label two or more transitions out of one state. One state is distinguished as the start state, and one or more states may be distinguished as accepting states or final states.

A non – deterministic finite automata (NDFA) recognizing the language (a|b)*abb is shown below:

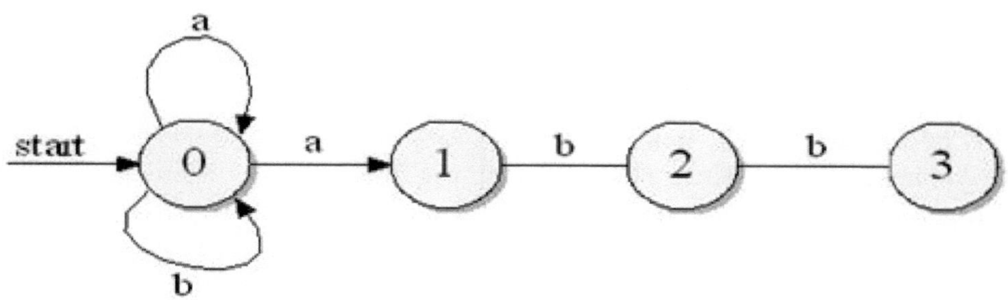

Fig. 12.2 NDFA Equivalent of the Regular Expression (a|b)*abb

The following is a transition table for the NFA shown above:

State	Input Symbols	
	a	b
0	{0, 1}	{0}
1	-	{2}
2	-	{3}

Fig. 12.3 Transition Table used for Converting NFA to DFA

In the transition table, there is a row for each state and a column for each admission input symbol and ε, if necessary. The entry for row i and symbol a is the set of possible next states for state i on input a.

The NFA accepts an input string x if and only if there is a path from the start state to some accepting state, such that the labels along that path spell out x. For example, the input strings abb, aabb, babb and aaabb are some of the strings accepted by the NFA mentioned above. Therefore the language defined by an NFA is the set of input strings it accepts.

Deterministic Finite Automation:

The automata, whose next state is uniquely given by the current state and the current input character is called Deterministic Finite Automata. In a FA, since δ defines mappings from Q*Σ to Q, there exists exactly one transition from a state on an input symbol; and therefore this finite automata is called as a Deterministic Finite Automata (DFA). Therefore, we can define the DFA as the Finite Automata: $M = (Q,\Sigma,\delta,q_0,F)$, such that there exists exactly one transition from a state on an input symbol.

A finite automation is deterministic if

1. It has no transition on input ε.
2. For each state s and input symbol a, there is almost one edge labeled a leaving s.

A deterministic version of a finite automation can be simulated in a straight forward manner, since a deterministic FA has almost one path from the start state labeled by any string.

Construct an NFA and a DFA for recognizing the language denoted by the regular expression aa* | bb*.

For each NFA we can find a DFA accepting the same language. Since there is at most one transition out of any state on any input symbol, a DFA is easier to simulate by a program than simulating an NFA. In reality the number of states of the DFA could be exponential than the number of states of the NFA, but in practice this worst case occurs rarely.

Advantages and Disadvantages of Transition Table Representation:

When describing a NFA, we use the transition graph representation. In a computer, the transition function of an NFA can be implemented in several different ways. The easiest implementation is a transition table in which there is a row for each state and a column for each input symbol and ε, if necessary.

The major advantage of using transition table representation is that it provides fast access to the transitions of a given state on a given character. On the other side, it can take up a lot of space when the input alphabet is large and most transitions are leading to empty sets.

If we are using a transition table to represent the transition function of a DFA, then each entry in the transition table is a single state. As a consequence, it is very easy to determine whether a deterministic finite automation accepts an input string, since there is at most one path from the start state labeled by that string.

Constructing a DFA from NFA:

The algorithm for constructing a DFA from an NFA is often called subset construction. The general idea behind this algorithm is that each DFA state corresponds to a set of NFA states. The DFA uses its state to keep track of all possible states the NFA can be in after reading each input symbol.

Using this algorithm, after reading input a1,a2,...an, the DFA is in a state that represents the subset T of the states of the NFA that are reachable from the NFA's start state along some path labeled a1,a2,....an.

The transformation from NFA to DFA involves the following steps:

i. Find all possible subsets of the set of states of the NFA.
ii. Consider each subset to be a state of the DFA
iii. Find the transition from it (the new state) on every input symbol.

All the states of a DFA obtained in this way might not be reachable from the initial state; and such states do not play a role in deciding what language is accepted by the DFA. Hence, the amount of work involved in transforming an NFA to DFA can be reduced if we attempt to generate only reachable states of a DFA.

For example consider the following finite automata:

$M = (\{q_0, q_1, q_2, q_3\}, \{0,1\}, \delta, q_0, \{q_3\})$

Where,

$\delta(q_0,0) = \{q_1\}$, $\delta(q_0,1) = \emptyset$

$\delta(q_1,0) = \{q_1\}$, $\delta(q_1,1) = \{q_1,q_2\}$

$\delta(q_2,0) = \emptyset$ $\delta(q_2,1) = \{q_3\}$

$\delta(q_3,0) = \{q_3\}$, $\delta(q_3,1) = \{q_3\}$

The transition table equivalent of the FA specified above is given below:

States	0	0
q_0	q_1	$\emptyset$
q_1	q_1	q_1,q_2
q_2	$\emptyset$	q_3
q_3	q_3	q_3

Fig. 12.4 Transition Table equivalent of the given FA

The DFA equivalent of the given NFA is represented in a transition table as follows:

		0	1
S_0	$\{q_0\}$	$\{q_1\}$	Ø
S_1	$\{q_1\}$	$\{q_1\}$	$\{q_1,q_2\}$
S_2	$\{q_1,q_2\}$	$\{q_1\}$	$\{q_1,q_2,q_3\}$
S_3	$\{q_1,q_2,q_3\}$	$\{q_1,q_3\}$	$\{q_1,q_2,q_3\}$
S_4	$\{q_1,q_3\}$	$\{q_1,q_3\}$	$\{q_1,q_2,q_3\}$
S_5	Ø	Ø	Ø

Fig. 12.5 Transition Table of DFA equivalent of NFA shown in Fig. 12.4

9 798887 338521

Printed by Libri Plureos GmbH in Hamburg,
Germany